PLANT FOSSILS

NATALIE
HYDE

Crabtree Publishing Company

www.crabtreebooks.com

Author
Natalie Hyde

Publishing plan research and development
Reagan Miller

Editor and indexer
Crystal Sikkens

Proofreader
Adrianna Morganelli

Design
Margaret Amy Salter

Photo research
Margaret Amy Salter, Crystal Sikkens

**Production coordinator
and prepress technician**
Samara Parent

Print coordinator
Margaret Amy Salter

Photographs
Associated Press: University of Florida/Dilcher: page 18
istockphoto: cover (background)
Science Source: Carlyn Iverson: page 6; Richard Bizley:
     page 22 (bottom); Richard Bizley: page23
Thinkstock: cover (foreground); pages 11, 15 (both), 16,
     26 (top right, middle left), 28 (bottom middle)
Wikimedia Commons: © Rene Sylvestersen: page 4; © John
     McColgan, Bureau of Land Management, Alaska Fire
     Service: page 7 (top); © Smith609: page 8; © Drawnnear:
     page 9 (top); © Ghedoghedo: page 9 (bottom); © RLKorotev:
     page 13 (top); © Ansgar Walk: page 17; © Tillman: page 19
     (bottom); © LadyofHats Mariana Ruiz: page 20; © Denis
     Barthel: page 21 (top); Jstuby: page 22 (top); © k2727: page 25
     (middle); Kevmin: page 26 (bottom left); © Steve46814: page
     26 (bottom right); © deror_avi: page 27; © Ardfern: page 28
     (top left)
All other images by Shutterstock

Library and Archives Canada Cataloguing in Publication

Hyde, Natalie, 1963-, author
         Plant fossils / Natalie Hyde.

(If these fossils could talk)
Includes index.
Issued in print and electronic formats.
ISBN 978-0-7787-1264-0 (bound).--ISBN 978-0-7787-1268-8
(pbk.).-- ISBN 978-1-4271-8958-5 (pdf).--ISBN 978-1-4271-8954-7
(html)

         1. Plants, Fossil--Juvenile literature. 2. Paleobotany--Juvenile
literature. I. Title.

QE906.H93 2013   j561   C2013-905237-2
                                                                    C2013-905238-0

Library of Congress Cataloging-in-Publication Data

Hyde, Natalie, 1963-
 Plant fossils / Natalie Hyde.
      pages cm. -- (If these fossils could talk)
 Includes index.
 ISBN 978-0-7787-1264-0 (reinforced library binding : alk. paper) -- ISBN
978-0-7787-1268-8 (pbk. : alk. paper) -- ISBN 978-1-4271-8958-5 (electronic
pdf : alk. paper) -- ISBN 978-1-4271-8954-7 (electronic html : alk. paper)
1. Plants, Fossil--Juvenile literature. I. Title.

 QE906.H94 2014
 561--dc23
                                                     2013033213

Crabtree Publishing Company

www.crabtreebooks.com   1-800-387-7650

Printed in Canada/092013/BF20130815

Copyright © **2014 CRABTREE PUBLISHING COMPANY**. All rights reserved. No part of this publication may be reproduced, stored in a
retrieval system or be transmitted in any form or by any means, electronic, mechanical, photocopying, recording, or otherwise, without the prior
written permission of Crabtree Publishing Company. In Canada: We acknowledge the financial support of the Government of Canada through the
Canada Book Fund for our publishing activities.

Published in Canada
Crabtree Publishing
616 Welland Ave.
St. Catharines, Ontario
L2M 5V6

Published in the United States
Crabtree Publishing
PMB 59051
350 Fifth Avenue, 59th Floor
New York, New York 10118

Published in the United Kingdom
Crabtree Publishing
Maritime House
Basin Road North, Hove
BN41 1WR

Published in Australia
Crabtree Publishing
3 Charles Street
Coburg North
VIC 3058

CONTENTS

PLANET OF PLANTS

Earth is a planet of plants. Without them, no life could exist here. The first plants were simple green algae that used photosynthesis to turn sunlight and water into food while creating oxygen. Oxygen is needed by almost every living thing, including humans.

RECORD OF PAST LIFE

Fossils are the remains of living things that have been preserved over time, and are our only direct record of past life on Earth. Plants have grown on every **continent** and every surface on the planet, and have left a large fossil record.

PLANT FOSSIL EXPERTS

Paleobotanists are scientists who study land and marine plant fossils. They use them to understand past climates, environments, and the evolution of plant life.

The cone that made this fossil fell to the ground around 55 million years ago.

ANCIENT MARINE PLANTS

The oldest plant fossil found so far is 580 million years old and was formed in an ancient sea in what is now China. The seaweed-like plant was about 1.5 inches (four centimeters) high and had a stalk and a crown of **tentacles**.

THE JUMP TO LAND

It took about 100 million more years before plants moved onto land. The first land plants were ferns and horsetails. Paleobotanists know this because of the fossilized **spores** they have found. Spores were how the first plants reproduced. These tiny grains were usually spread by water or wind.

*It took about another 200 million years for flowering plants, such as maple, oak, and apple trees, and grains such as wheat and barley, to **evolve**.*

spores

A close-up of this fern shows its spores.

NOTEWORTHY NAMES

Kaspar Maria von Sternberg known as the "father of paleobotany," lived in Prague, Czech Republic. He used to search the coal mines near his home for plant fossils. His collection of fossils became the core collection at the National Museum in Prague.

FIRST FOSSILS

Even though Earth was covered with plant life of one kind or another for millions of years, the fossil record of the earliest plants is poor. The first plants were small and made of soft tissue. This material would disintegrate long before it could become fossilized.

TOUGHEN UP!

Like other fossils, plant fossils are found in **sedimentary rocks**. Plants would be covered with silt, clay, or mud at the bottom of streams or lakes. Over time layers and layers of sediment build up and the pressure turns the layers to rock. The plant will often decay, but will leave an imprint called a mold. Sometimes minerals collect in the mold and harden. This creates a fossil called a cast.

The top leaf fossil in this picture is a mold. The bottom one is a cast.

ROCK HARD

Thick woody parts of plants, such as tree trunks, sometimes fell into water where minerals could seep in. The mineralized wood kept all the details of the living plant, which is an important source of information for paleobotanists.

STICKY TRAP

Some plant material is found in amber, which is fossilized tree resin. When this resin seeps out of trees, it is sticky and plant and animal material could be caught in it and preserved for millions of years.

*Fire normally destroys plant material, but sometimes some details are preserved in the **charcoal** that remains.*

FACT FILE

Most plants often break apart. Pinecones fall to the ground or plants shed leaves, flower petals, and seeds. This means that most plant fossils are just part of a plant. This makes naming plant fossils a bit of a challenge. Often different parts of plants are assigned different names, even though they came from the same plant.

How is a cast fossil different from a mold fossil?

FROM SEA TO LAND

In the beginning our planet was a barren, rocky place. The first plants still lived in the water and were simple algae. Sometimes these algae plants grew together to form algal mats on the bottom of shallow water. Creatures would burrow down into the mats and get stuck. These layers of algae are an important source of animal fossils for paleontologists.

DARING EXPLORER

Liverworts are believed to be one of the first plants that moved from sea to land. They did not have stems or roots, just flat ribbon-like leaves. Fossil liverwort spores that have been found in Argentina are the oldest land-plant fossil found to date—about 472 million years old!

STEM SOLUTION

As plants developed cells that could transport water up a stem, they were able to move into drier areas. Fossils of one of the first very simple land plants, called *Cooksonia*, were found in Ireland.

Cooksonia *had a stem that branched out with little balls on the end where spores formed.*

ROOTS AND LEAVES

Clubmosses were a small step ahead of *Cooksonia* because they had not only branching stems, but also simple roots and needle-like leaves. Over time, clubmosses grew to be as tall as trees!

MORE SPORES

Spores make up most of the fossil record for these early plants. Spores have tough walls and are light so they can be spread easily by wind and water. Their walls help protect them from weather and bacteria, which make them good material for fossilization.

NOTEWORTHY NAMES Isabel Clifton Cookson was an Australian botanist who specialized in paleobotany. Her work with plant fossils helped develop theories of early land-plant evolution.

clubmoss

This fossil shows a Cooksonia *plant fossil. The* Cooksonia *was named in honor of Isabel Cookson.*

A STICKY SOLUTION

Resin is a clear, sticky substance that seeps out of many plants, but mostly evergreen trees. As it ages, resin becomes yellow and hard. Anything caught in the sticky goo is trapped forever.

GOLDEN TREASURE

Amber is a very valuable fossil for paleobotanists. It is a plant fossil itself and gives information on the evolution of trees that produce resin. It has also preserved all kinds of plant material. Many plant **inclusions**, such as flowers, seeds, and leaves are often too delicate to survive other kinds of fossilization. In amber, the tiniest details are visible.

GET A CLUE

Even amber that doesn't contain any plant material is valuable to paleobotanists. Sometimes the native plants in the area could be determined by the insects trapped in amber. For instance, fig wasps only develop in figs and point to that kind of tree being in the area.

Seeds, spores, and other plant parts are trapped in this amber which was made into a bracelet.

Scientists think amber resin helped the tree prevent bacteria or insects from entering openings in the stem or trunk.

MAKE MINE A COMBO

The combination of plant and animal material together in amber is important, too. A bee trapped in amber that is carrying pollen from an orchid on its back tells paleobotanists two things: even without fossils of delicate orchid flowers, they have a clue as to how long ago the plant developed. Also, the way the pollen was stuck to the bee's back showed that the flower was bell-shaped.

FOSSIL FUNGUS

Scientists have found a 52-million-year-old piece of amber that shows the special relationship between fungus and plants. Even that long ago fungus grew on plant roots to help them get **nutrients** from the soil.

FACT FILE

Long ago, people thought amber had magical and healing powers. People wore amber amulets to protect them from diseases such as gout, toothaches, and sore throats.

FOSSILS IN COAL

The thick forests that once covered Earth didn't just disappear. The remains of these plants are one of the most important natural resources we have today. Coal is a brownish-black sedimentary rock made from ancient plants. Coal is burned around the world to produce heat and energy.

COAL FROM PLANTS

Ancient plants that lived in wet areas would eventually fall into the water and be covered by sediment. The mud and acidic water kept them from **decomposing**. As more layers piled up, the remains of plants on the bottom were pressed together and heated. This turned the material into peat. With more time and pressure the peat became coal.

Coal is called a fossil fuel because it is made from the remains of dead plants, but it is not a true fossil because the plants were changed into another material.

COAL BALLS

Sometimes plant material is preserved as a fossil in a coal ball. Like their name, coal balls are usually round and when paleobotanists cut and peel them they can examine the ancient tissue of plants that would otherwise have been destroyed.

coal ball

coal seam

FOSSIL FOREST

Sometimes good plant fossils can be found in the layers between **coal seams**. Recently scientists discovered a 300-million-year-old fossilized rain forest on the ceiling of a coal mine in Illinois. The fossil forest was buried when an earthquake lowered the ground and a river flooded the ground. Paleobotanists found clubmosses over 100 feet (30 meters) tall towering over horsetails and seed ferns.

NOTEWORTHY NAMES

Reinhardt Thiessen is a coal paleobotanist. By identifying the fossil spores in coal, he was able to understand what kind of forests created the coal seam. He figured out how well it would burn based on what plant material it was made of.

SOWING SEEDS

Seed plants are now the most common type of plant on Earth. They outnumber all other plant groups and grow in almost every environment on Earth. Seed plants affect the lives of every other living thing.

SEEDLINGS

From seed-bearing plants we get paper and lumber, food such as grains, fruits, and vegetables, and food for animals, such as corn and grasses. Materials found in seed plants are also used to make medicines, oils, and perfumes.

ANCIENT SEEDS

The earliest seed plants were very small and did not grow seeds in cones or flowers. Their seeds were in a little cup-like structure along their branches. The oldest seed fossil, which is 360 million years old, shows three 0.2 inch (five mm) long seeds inside a cup-like structure.

We use cotton from the cotton seed plant to make clothing.

A GREAT IDEA

Plants develop seeds as a way of protecting the newly formed plant. The seed contains the plant embryo, or undeveloped plant, and a hard outer shell to protect it. This strong coating helps seeds survive fossilization.

CONE ZONE

Cycads, an ancient type of seed plant, are the **ancestor** of evergreen coniferous trees, such as pines, spruces, and firs. Cycads develop a cone to protect their seeds. The cone opens so insects can get in when the seeds are ready to be **pollinated**. After, it closes again to protect the developing seeds.

Cycads developed about 145 to 200 million years ago, and some types are still around today!

closed cycad

open cycad

FACT FILE

A fossil site called the Messel Pit, in Germany, is an old shale quarry. Shale is a type of sedimentary rock. So many fossils have been found at the Messel Pit that it has been named a UNESCO World Heritage site. Fossilized seeds found there show how plants developed different strategies to spread their seeds. Some seeds have wings to be carried by the wind. Some are meant to be carried by animals, and other plants have exploding **capsules** that scatter the seeds over a wide area.

A TOUGH EXTERIOR

Some of the best preserved plant fossils are from the woody parts of plants such as bark or tree trunks. These large sturdy structures took longer to decompose and therefore had a better chance of becoming fossilized.

TREE TRUNKS

Fossils of tree trunks show that ancient trees had very different bark. Many had a diamond or scale pattern that looked a little like alligator skin. These scars were made as leaves **detached** from the trunk as the tree grew. Some fossil tree trunks also show growth rings just like modern trees.

PETRIFIED WOOD

Some tree trunks that fell into water were covered with sediment and did not decompose. Minerals in the water would seep into the trunk's cells turning the wood into rock. The rock, called petrified wood, would still have its original shape and details.

Sometimes minerals would preserve large amounts of trees, creating a petrified forest.

MUMMIFIED FOREST

High in the Canadian Arctic are the remains of a 45-million-year-old forest. The tree trunks, leaves, and seedpods were not turned to stone like other fossils. They were mummified, or dried out, and preserved by the cold, dry arctic air and covered with sediment. Floods **unearthed** the mummified forest and paleobotanists were amazed that once they thawed the wood, it could be cut, shaped, and burned as if it had been growing only months before. Mummified plant material is important because the cells have not been replaced by minerals and scientists can see exactly how the plant looked and grew.

How is mummified wood different from petrified wood?

The 45-million-year-old mummified trees on Axel Heiberg Island were about 75 years old when they died. But scientists believe they had a short growing season.

FLOWER POWER

Flower fossils are rare because flowers easily and quickly decompose before they can fossilize. The few that have been found were between layers of rock or in charcoal.

FINDING CLUES
Flower fossils give paleobotanists an idea of the climate of the area as well as what types of insects might have lived nearby to pollinate the plant. Flower fossils found without leaves cause problems for scientists because they are not sure whether the flower belonged to a tree, shrub, or vine.

UNDER THE SEA
One of the oldest, most complete flowering plant fossils was found in China. It was a plant that was about 20 inches (50 cm) high and it probably lived under water. The flower did not have petals, but paleobotanists found seeds inside unripe fruit.

The oldest flowering plant fossil is thought to be more than 125 million years old.

PLANT PARENTS

A rare plant fossil was found in northern Argentina. It is an early relative of the *Asteraceae* family, which includes daisies, sunflowers, chrysanthemums, lettuce, and artichokes. The fossil was pressed between layers of rocks about 47 million years old. It is helping paleobotanists understand how the sunflower family evolved and how it spread.

This 300-million-year-old fern leaf looks very similar to the leaves on fern plants today.

NEW OR OLD?

Leaf fossils are more common than flower fossils because trees typically shed thousands of leaves each year. While many fossilized leaves look very similar to leaves of modern trees, others have strange shapes and structures and measure almost six feet (two meters) long!

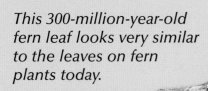

 **FACT FILE** Paleobotanists made an interesting discovery in Idaho. Pressed between layers of sediment that had turned to stone were un-decomposed leaves. If you split the rock open, the leaves are still there—mummified!

MEAT-EATING PLANTS

Carnivorous plants are plants that get most of their food from eating animals. Although these plants use their leaves to catch sunlight for photosynthesis, their leaves are also used as traps to catch insects. Inside the traps is a liquid that digests the insect, giving food to the plant.

Scientists believe the ancient pitcher plant grow to be two inches (five cm) high.

FEW FOSSILS

Carnivorous plants were made mostly of water. When the plants dried out they were as light as a feather and easily broke apart. They did not fossilize well and most information about them comes from fossilized seeds and pollen.

PITCHER PERFECT

A 100-million-year-old fossil found in China shows a plant with leaf "pitchers," or cups, spiraling around its stem. It resembles the modern pitcher plant. The fossil pitchers have spoon-shaped lids, which glowed yellow-green around their edges.

SNAP TRAP

Fossilized seeds from another carnivorous plant were found in Europe. They grew there when the climate was warmer and wetter. The *Aldrovanda* was a water plant that had snap traps at the end of its leaf **whorls**. When it sensed prey, or animals eaten as food, the bristles at the end of the leaf would close, trapping its meal.

ANCIENT SUNDEWS

Paleobotanists have also discovered fossilized pollen from an ancestor of the sundew family in Taiwan and India. *Droserapollis* had leaves that had tentacle-like ends covered in sticky liquid that looked like a drop of dew.

Like the ancient Droserapollis, *the modern sundew attracts insects by their "dewdrops." Once an insect touches it they are stuck. The leaf then curls around the prey and digests it.*

leaf whorls

The Aldrovanda Vesiculosa *(above) is the only surviving species from the ancient* Aldrovanda *plants.*

What plant and leaf structures are possible evidence of a carnivorous plant?

MEGAFLORA

If you stood in a prehistoric forest or jungle, you would be amazed at what you saw. Some plants reached an enormous size. Scientists are not sure why some past plants became giants.

Scale trees had diamond patterned bark.

Calamites grew as high as 120 feet (36 m). Scale trees grew even taller—they soared to a height of 150 feet (45 m).

calamite

scale trees

COLOSSAL CALAMITES

The calamite was a prehistoric tree that is related to the horsetail plant of today. Fossils show that it had a stem with lines that looked a lot like bamboo and whorls at the end of its branches.

LARGE SCALE

Scale trees grew in wet areas 300 million years ago. They were related to the small clubmosses. Scale trees reproduced using spores kept in cones. These cones could be 1.5 feet (50 cm) long and contain eight billion spores!

Some ferns had leaves that were ten feet (three m) long.

TOWERING FERNS

Ferns are a common houseplant, but 300 million years ago ferns were the size of trees that grew 32 feet (ten m) high. They had a long stem and leaves only at the top, making them look a little like a modern palm tree.

THEORIES, PLEASE

There are several theories as to why plants grew to a giant size in the past. Warmer, wetter climates may have provided the perfect growing environment. Plenty of carbon dioxide in the air may have also played a part.

FACT FILE

The opposite of megaflora fossils are microfossils. These are the tiny remains of living things. Spores and pollen are typical plant microfossils. They need special handling because of the dangerous acids and high-powered microscopes needed to study them.

PLANT OR ANIMAL?

Some fossils are difficult to identify because they belong to **ancient** organisms **that have no living relatives. The earliest life-forms manufactured food from the Sun using photosynthesis like plants, and moved and reproduced in water like animals.**

A LITTLE OF BOTH

Cyanobacteria are an example of an organism leading this double life. They lived in shallow seas long before there were any plants or animals. They are in fact the oldest fossils we know, more than 3.5 billion years old! More surprising, this group of bacteria are still living today.

(below) Cyanobacteria, shown here among minerals and algae in Yellowstone National Park, are one of the largest and most important groups of bacteria on Earth.

OXYGEN-MAKERS

These organisms use the Sun to create their own food, just like plants do. By taking in carbon dioxide and giving off oxygen, cyanobacteria changed the **atmosphere** on our planet making it full of oxygen to support new life.

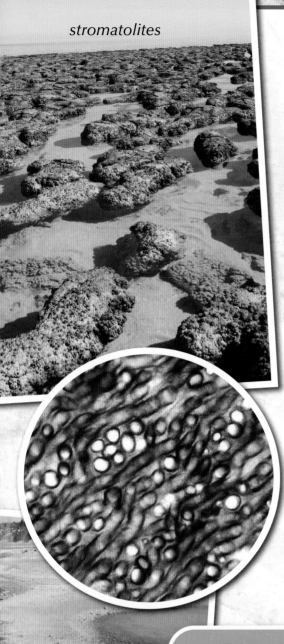

stromatolites

STONE PILLARS

Even though cyanobacteria are only one cell, they often grow in colonies large enough for us to see them. Stromatolites are rocky columns formed by the remains of cyanobacteria. Some stromatolites are still being formed today in shallow coastal waters in Australia.

FOSSIL FUNGUS

Fungi are neither plants nor animals, but are in a group all their own. They are like plants because they are often found in forests and cannot move on their own. But like animals, they get their nutrients from other living things.

Fungi fossils are usually so tiny they can only be seen under a microscope. Very few large fungi fossils, such as mushrooms, have been found.

FACT FILE

A fossil found in China recently is causing problems for paleontologists. This 600-million-year-old fossil doesn't look like any organism living today. Some of its features point to the organism being a type of seaweed. Other details resemble sea sponges or sea anemones. Scientists still aren't sure whether it is a plant or animal.

LIVING FOSSILS

Sometimes we see a plant in the fossil record that looks just like the species living today. These amazing plants survived the major extinction events and did not change much over millions of years. We call these "living fossils."

monkey puzzle trees

STILL THE SAME

The *Ginkgo biloba* is a tall tree native to China. The tree has no close living relatives. Some of the oldest living trees are thought to be up to 1,500 years old. Fossils of *Ginkgo biloba* leaves can be up to 270 million years old and look identical to the leaves today.

modern Ginkgo biloba *leaf*

Ginkgo biloba *leaves are bright green in the summer and turn a golden yellow in autumn.*

49-million-year-old Ginkgo biloba leaf fossil

Ginko biloba tree

MONKEY PUZZLE

On the slopes of the Andes Mountains in Chile and Argentina grows a living fossil called the monkey puzzle tree. It has sharp, armor-like leaves that caused an Englishman to once say that it would be a puzzle for a monkey to climb. That's how it got its name. It still looks the same as the monkey puzzle trees that fossilized 160 million years ago.

When the Wollemi Pine was first discovered, scientists couldn't identify it until they looked at the fossil record and found its ancestors.

FAMOUS FIND

In 1994, in a remote area of Wollemi National Park in Australia, a tree was discovered that scientists believed was extinct. It is called the Wollemi Pine, and it is listed as critically endangered because fewer than 100 trees remain.

FACT FILE

Russian scientists have brought back to life a 32,000-year-old plant (*Silene stenopylla*) whose seeds were found frozen in Siberia. The seeds were probably stored by an ice age squirrel. They were surrounded by wooly mammoth and wooly rhinoceros bones. The plant has now grown and produced its own seeds creating a new "living fossil."

AMBER BUG BRITTLE

Ask an adult to help with this activity. You will be making your own bug-filled amber that is good enough to eat! You will need:

2 cups (473 ml) white sugar

2 cups (473 ml) water

yellow and red food coloring

gummy worms and/or gummy bugs

saucepan

Optional: flavor extract, such as lemon, orange, or root beer

cookie sheet

wax paper

wooden spoon

1. Combine the sugar and water in a saucepan.

2. With an adult, cook over medium heat until the sugar dissolves and creates a thick, syrupy mixture.

3. Add about 12 drops of yellow food coloring into the mixture. Now add 3 or 4 drops of red food coloring until you get a dark yellow or deep orange color.

4. Add a few drops of the flavor extract of your choice, if you wish.

5. Line a cookie sheet with wax paper. Have an adult pour the hot sugar mixture onto wax paper.

6. Drop gummy bugs into the sugar mixture and push them in using the back of a wooden spoon. Careful! Don't touch the mixture because it will be hot.

7. Let cool overnight. Lift the wax paper up from the cookie sheet and crack the hard sugar amber into pieces.

8. Enjoy!

Be sure an adult is there to help you when working with a hot stove.

GLOSSARY

algae A group of small plants containing chlorophyll

ancestors An early type of animal or plant from which others have evolved

atmosphere The gases surrounding Earth

barren Having no plants

capsules Small cases or containers

charcoal A black material produced when wood is burned

coal seam A layer of coal in the ground

continent A large landmass

cupule

decomposing Decaying; rotting away

detached Separated from

disintegrate Break into very small parts

evolve To grow or develop slowly

extinction The dying out of a species

inclusions Material that is trapped inside something else

nutrients Chemicals needed by organisms to live and grow

organisms Any living plants or animals

paleontologists People who study fossils of plants, animals, and other organisms

photosynthesis The process plants use to turn sunlight, carbon dioxide, and water into food

pollinated A plant fertilized with pollen. Once plants are pollinated they can make seeds.

sedimentary rocks Rocks created from layers of material such as silt or clay

spores A small plant part capable of growing into new plants

tentacles A long, thin part of a plant or animal

unearthed Something found in the ground by digging

whorl Three or more leaves or petals that circle a stem

LEARNING MORE

FURTHER READING:

Bonner, Hannah. *When Bugs Were Big, Plants Were Strange, and Tetrapods Stalked the Earth.* National Geographic Children's Books, 2004.

Connors, Kathleen. *Plant fossils.* Gareth Stevens Publishing, 2012.

Dixon, Dougal. T*he Illustrated Encyclopedia of Prehistoric Life.* Hamlyn Young Books, 1992.

McNamara, Ken. *We Came from Slime!* Annick Press, 2006.

WEBSITES:

Gardening for kids with prehistoric plants:
www.kidsgardening.org/node/12087

A plant fossil picture gallery:
www.paleoportal.org/index.php

All about fossils from the San Diego Natural History Museum:
www.sdnhm.org/archive/kids/fossils/index.html

Pictures and information about living fossils:
http://webecoist.momtastic.com/2009/12/29/living-fossils-10-plants-animals-with-staying-power/

INDEX